CONTENTS

INTRODUCTION
TO SOCIAL MEDIA

Social media, according to the *Oxford English Dictionary*, are websites and applications (apps) "that enable users to create and share content or to participate in social networking." Apps are typically accessed on mobile devices like smartphones or tablets.

Social media platforms like Facebook and Twitter allow people to keep up with the lives of friends and family members, stay in touch with acquaintances who live all over the globe, and access news and information about things that interest them, even if those interests are of narrow focus to mainstream media outlets.

Do you enjoy creating bird designs in needlepoint? You can find hundreds of others who share the same passion and would love to share their work on Facebook or Pinterest. Does your idea of "retirement" involve exploring the country in a motor home? It's easy to connect with others in that community, whether it's just to share photos on Instagram or use Twitter to log your travels. There is truly something for everyone when it comes to social media.

About 70 percent of Americans use at least some form of social media on a regular basis, the Pew Research Center reported in 2017. Among those in the 18–29 age group, that percentage hovers in the 85–90 range. It is worth noting, though, that social media usage among older Americans has grown rapidly in recent years— about two-thirds in the 50–64 age group, and at least

ABOUT EMAIL

Email, or electronic mail, is an easy way to send and receive messages over the internet. Instead of requiring a physical address, a stamp, and the few to several days it takes for a letter to travel, email uses an address that contains the AT SIGN (@) and can transmit your message instantly—and free, save for the fee you pay to your Internet service provider.

Create your Google Account

One account is all you need
One free account gets you into everything Google.

G M ⬛ ▶ ⬥ ⬦ ▷ ⬡

Take it all with you
Switch between devices and pick up wherever you left off.

Name
First | Last

Choose your username
@gmail.com

Create a password

Confirm your password

Birthday
Month | Day | Year

Gender
I am...

Mobile phone

SIGNING UP FOR GMAIL

Go to Gmail.com and click the *Create Account* button. You will be prompted to fill in some information, including a username that ends in "@gmail.com." This will be your email address.

Once you've set up an account, getting started is as easy as clicking *Compose*. A new message will appear—think of this as the stationery for your letter. Simply type the email address of the intended recipient in the top field of the message window labeled *To*. Unlike physical mail, email allows you to send to multiple people at once, even if they don't all live in the same place. You may add several addresses to this field.

The *Subject* field is the place to type a brief description of your topic. For example, you might type "Happy Birthday" if sending birthday wishes to a friend. The large white space under the *Subject* field is where your message goes. It can be as long or short as you wish. You can also attach electronic files such as photos or documents by clicking the PAPER CLIP icon at the bottom of the message window.

When finished, hit *Send*. Your email should be waiting for the recipient to open in his or her inbox!

OTHER EMAIL ACCOUNT PROVIDERS

OUTLOOK MAIL
SITE: Outlook.com
example@outlook.com

YAHOO MAIL
SITE: Mail.yahoo.com
example@yahoo.com

AOL MAIL
SITE: Mail.aol.com
example@aol.com

ZOHO MAIL
SITE: Zoho.com
example@zoho.com

WHAT IS FACEBOOK?

Facebook, founded in 2004, has more than one billion active users worldwide. It's an easy way to keep up with old friends, connect with new ones, and share the things that are important to you with those in your network.

Facebook's almost universally recognized LIKE icon.

Sign Up

It's free and always will be.

First name | Last name

Mobile number or email

New password

Birthday

Nov | 20 | 1992 | Why do I need to provide my birthday?

○ Female ○ Male

By clicking Create Account, you agree to our **Terms** and that you have read our **Data Policy**, including our **Cookie Use**. You may receive SMS Notifications from Facebook and can opt out at any time.

Create Account

SIGNING UP FOR FACEBOOK

Getting started on Facebook is free and easy. Simply go to Facebook.com and fill in your information under the header *Sign Up*. Once you've finished and click the *Create Account* button, you will be prompted to add a profile photo (usually a close-up photo of yourself), a cover photo (a larger picture that can be of you, your family, or anything that appeals to you), and information about your life and interests. You may be as detailed as you like, or you can simply start with the basics. A photo is imperative, though, as it will allow your friends to know they are connecting with the right person when they look up your profile.

C   🔒 Secure | https://www.facebook.com

f   Search   Q   Marty   Home   👥 ● ●   ❓ ▾

The **TRIANGLE** icon on the right side of the Tool Bar will give you access to various settings and preferences for your profile. Under the **GLOBE** icon you can view all of your notifications from friends who you are following or who have tagged you in a post. The **CHAT BUBBLE** icon is where you can create and send new Private Messages (PMs), and it also contains all of your PMs. The **SILHOUETTE** icon to the left of that will show you all of your pending Friend Requests. The *Home* button will take you back to your Newsfeed, as will the **FACEBOOK** icon to the left of the search bar. Your **PROFILE** icon with your name next to it will take you to your profile and your wall where you can view all of your activity and also edit your profile.

Marty   ✎ Edit Profile

You can update or change anything in your Facebook profile at any time—including your photos. It's quite common for Facebook users to update their profile and cover photos regularly. To edit your Profile, go to your Profile page and click the *Edit Profile* button that will appear near the bottom of your cover photo.

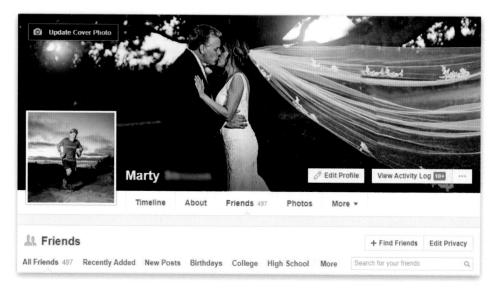

FINDING FACEBOOK FRIENDS

Making the most of Facebook requires "becoming Facebook friends" with the people in your life, whether they're family, friends, or long-lost acquaintances. There are many ways to do so. To get started, click the *Friends* button near the top of your profile page. Then click the *+Find Friends* button that will appear below your photo. That will take you to a screen where Facebook provides several options.

You can simply search by name, or by several other criteria including hometown, employer, or school. Once you find someone you'd like to friend, simply click the *Add Friend* button next to their name and profile picture. They will be notified of your request.

There are various fields you can use to search for people you know.

A Notification showing this Facebook user has one pending Friend Request.

Once they accept, the two of you will be Facebook friends. And now that you're on Facebook, you can be certain you will also be receiving notifications from those who want to friend you, too! When sending or receiving these requests, it's a smart idea to click on the person's profile to make sure it's who you think it is.

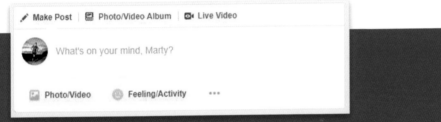

UPDATING YOUR FACEBOOK STATUS

The items that appear as you scroll down your Facebook home page make up what's called your Newsfeed. Primarily, you will see photos and status updates from your friends. Keeping up with these is what Facebook is all about! And you can make it a two-way conversation by commenting on or liking their status with the LIKE icon. You can update your own status and add photos to your Timeline that will appear in your friends' Newsfeeds. Near the top of the page is an area that makes it easy to do so. To update your status, just type what you'd like to say in the box. For example, "So excited that I just set up my own Facebook account!" There's a button to add photos or video, too.

WHAT IS TWITTER?

Twitter has been around since 2006 and now has more than 300 million monthly users. It allows users to contribute and keep up with the conversation of Tweets, which are short snippets of text and/or photos and videos about any number of topics. Twitter is a great way to keep up with news and information about specific topics that interest you.

SIGNING UP FOR TWITTER

Signing up is very easy. Visit Twitter.com, and click the *Sign Up* link at the top of the page. You will need to

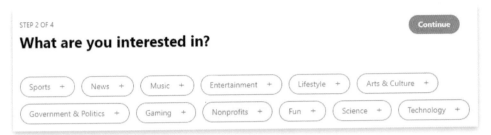

STEP 2 OF 4

What are you interested in?

Continue

(Sports +) (News +) (Music +) (Entertainment +) (Lifestyle +) (Arts & Culture +)

(Government & Politics +) (Gaming +) (Nonprofits +) (Fun +) (Science +) (Technology +)

Upon signup, Twitter will suggest a number of subjects you are interested in to start connecting you with others.

give your full name and email address, and then will be prompted to choose a Twitter name, or your Handle. Including your real name somewhere in your Twitter name might help friends find you, but you might need to add numbers or another word since no two users can have the same name.

I-FI

◎ Chicago, IL

🔗

📅 Joined July 2017

○ Born on August 1, 1986

🖼 7 Photos and videos

CREATING A BIO

Building a bio will help Twitter show you Tweets that will be of interest to you. Once you have chosen your handle, you will be asked to identify topics that interest you. After you make your selections and press the **Continue** button, Twitter will offer to find friends for you using your email account. Allowing this will help you find others you know who use Twitter. This makes it easy to see their Tweets. Twitter will make recommendations on people it thinks you should follow, based on your contacts and the interests you expressed. But it's important to note that who you follow is up to you!

THE BASICS OF TWITTER

Tweets can be (and are) about anything and everything. The key to making the most of Twitter will be finding users whose Tweets interest you. Simply click the *Follow* button and their Tweets will then show up on your Twitter home page. That's a great way to keep up with people and topics you're interested in.

RETWEETING AND HASHTAGS

In addition to giving you a place to express your own Tweets and read those from others, Twitter also allows you to spread the word on items you find interesting by Retweeting them. By hitting the Retweet icon, you can share a Tweet from someone else with those who follow you. You can also add your own thoughts to the Retweet.

It's #museumselfieday! 📸

💭 First selfie ever? 🤳 We bet photographers Joseph Byron and Ben Falk (holding the camera on the left & right) wouldn't mind having the honor of that title! 🏆

[Byron Company, 1920; MCNY, 93.1.4.18]

If you will be joining the conversation by doing your own Tweeting, another key will be staying within the character limits. Twitter was set up to be a series of very quick reads. It's not the place for long-form writing!

Another tool helpful in finding Tweets of interest is called the Hashtag. Using what's commonly known as the POUND SIGN (#), you can Tag a topic to the end of a Tweet that will allow others to find that Tweet. Using the Museum of the City of New York's Tweet as an example, a user who searches Twitter for the Hashtag used by the museum (by typing *#museumselfieday* in the search box at the top of the page) will be able to find other Tweets containing the same Hashtag.

You can also Tag other Twitter users in your Tweets by using their Handles preceded by the AT SIGN (@). For example, if you wanted to Tag the Museum of the City of New York in a Tweet you were posting, you would simply include *@MuseumofCityNY* in your Tweet. This will then notify the museum that they have been mentioned in a conversation.

WHAT IS SNAPCHAT?

Launched in 2011, Snapchat soared in popularity largely for its technology that allowed users to send photos that would, within seconds, "disappear" from the recipient. That is, the photos could be seen temporarily but not saved permanently. Snapchat has evolved into a popular way to stay connected on the go, through photos, videos, and even text updates.

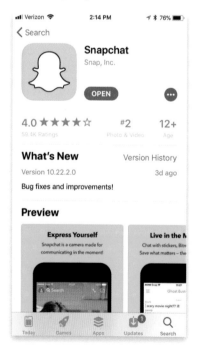

GETTING STARTED ON SNAPCHAT

The first thing to note about Snapchat is that it is meant to be used from your mobile device. To get started, you need to

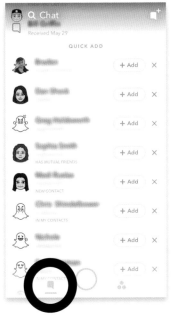

download the Snapchat app on your smartphone or tablet. Once you've done that, getting signed up is easy. Simply open the app and follow the prompts in giving your name and email address, and in choosing a Handle, or username.

By tapping on the **CHAT BUBBLE** icon of the at the bottom of the screen, you can find people in the contact list of your mobile device who are on Snapchat. By clicking the **+Add** button next to a name, you can add contacts with whom you might want to share snaps.

SHARING SNAPS

Sharing snaps can be as easy as taking a photo within the app. As soon as you do, an **ARROW** icon will appear at the bottom of the screen that will allow you to send the snap to someone. There are also icons along the right that allow you to add text to your snap, to draw on it, to add effects to the snap, and to adjust the length of time the snap will display. Once you hit the **ARROW** icon to send your Snap, you will be prompted to choose the person or people you would like to receive your snap.

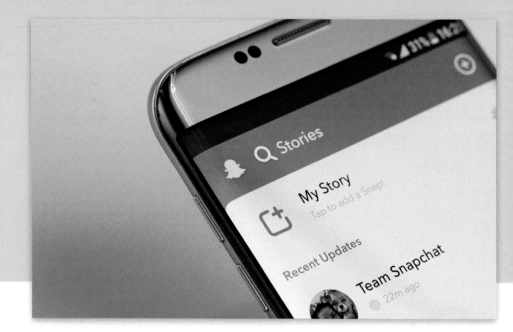

SNAPCHAT STORIES

In addition to sending Snaps to your contacts, Snapchat allows you to create Stories that include a series of Snaps. You can choose to share these stories with everyone, with a certain group of your contacts, or even to groups of people located in your geographic vicinity.

When you go to send a Snap and click the **CREATE A STORY** icon, you will be asked what type of Story you would like to create. Stories are a great way to share a sequence of events in pictures, such as a vacation.

MORE SNAPCHAT FEATURES

Exploring Snapchat will lead you to a treasure trove of fun features. Below are just a few of them to help you on your journey.

Score: Your Snapchat score is the result of a special formula that gives you credit for the number of Snaps you have sent and received, Stories you have posted, and other factors that measure your usage of the

A Snapchat vending machine in L.A. that sells Snapchat's new Spectacles, a pair of photographic smartglasses that sync with your phone to to take photos and videos to share on Snapchat.

app. Don't worry too much about it as you're getting started, but the more engaged you are the higher your score will be.

Snapcode: An easy way to add contacts on Snapchat is by using the camera mode to take a photo of someone else's Snapcode.

Geofilter: By allowing Snapchat to know your location, you can access Filters to enhance your Snaps. Simply take a photo and then swipe left. Some geographical areas and major attractions offer several Snapchat filters you can select.

Snapcodes not only make adding friends an easier process, but they can allow you to unlock Filters, Lenses, and even access exclusive content.

You can also save your Stories to your Memories if you have a sequence of Snaps you want to save for later. This builds a library of Memories that you can access and

WHAT IS INSTAGRAM?

Instagram took off in 2010 as a popular way for users to instantly share photos and videos with their friends. Because it is built almost exclusively on images and video shot with smartphones, it is best enjoyed by downloading the free app on a mobile device.

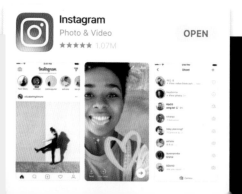

Instagram is great way to show your friends your life through pictures. You can connect with friends, media outlets, and your favorite companies to stay up to date with everything you care about.

GETTING STARTED WITH INSTAGRAM

As with most social media apps, getting started is quick and simple. Locate the free app, download it to your phone, and walk through the easy set-up process that will require you to give your email address and decide on a Handle—the name that will appear when you share photos or comment on the photos of others.

FOLLOWING AND BEING FOLLOWED

The key to making the most of your time on Instagram is finding a group of people to follow—your family and friends, of course, along with others whose photos and videos you find interesting. When you sign up for Instagram, you will be given options to connect with people from your email account, your Facebook account, and other social media services you might use. It's a great idea to follow at least some people you know. They will see that you have chosen to follow you, and could decide to follow you in return. That means they will be able to view and comment on the photos and videos you share.

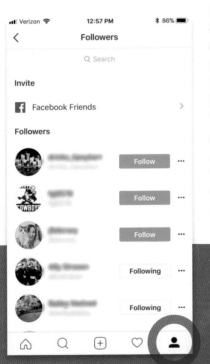

You can look for additional people to follow at any time by clicking the PROFILE icon at the bottom of the screen.

INSTAGRAM TIPS

In addition to the **PROFILE** icon referenced on the previous page, there are four

other main navigational buttons at the bottom of the screen. The middle **PLUS SIGN (+)** icon is your primary trigger to share photos and videos with your followers. That icon will allow you to take a photo or video to share on the spot, or to access the camera roll on your phone so you can share a photo or video you have already taken.

FILTERING PHOTOS

As soon as you take a photo, a series of filters will appear at the

bottom of the screen. You can scroll through them and tap any one to see how that effect will look on your masterpiece.

TAGGING OTHER USERS

If someone you follow on Instagram appears in your photo, you can also Tag that person by tapping on their image and choosing their name. Once you are satisfied with your picture or video, clicking the **SHARE** icon will allow those who follow you to see it!

EXPLORING INSTAGRAM

The **HOME** icon in the bottom left corner allows you to see the latest shares from those you follow. The **MAGNIFYING GLASS** icon next to that allows you to search by name, subject, or any keyword for photos and videos from all over. Finally, the **HEART** icon lets you see who has started following you, along with who has liked or commented on your photos and

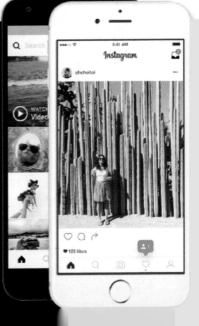

WHAT IS LINKEDIN?

LinkedIn is the professional's social media platform. That is, while the likes of Snapchat and Instagram were built for the sharing of personal lives through photos and video, LinkedIn is the destination for employers and employees to network.

Go to Linkedin.com to get started. Here, you will use your actual name—rather than a username—to identify yourself. You will also, of course, need to provide a valid email address.

That's all there is to getting signed up, but making effective use of the platform requires a little more time and diligence.

CREATING A STRONG PROFILE

After signing up, you will be guided through a series of questions designed to strengthen your profile. LinkedIn even provides a profile strength indicator to show you how yours stacks up.

Of course, some aspects of a strong profile are a given. Use a professional-looking headshot as your profile photo, rather than a candid shot or action picture. Be sure to give a thorough listing of your current job, your experience, skills, education, and areas of expertise. Other LinkedIn users might take a keen interest in your resume if looking for job candidates, guest speakers, or just to add knowledgeable contacts.

In addition to letting you know how strong it considers your profile, LinkedIn will inform you—in the Notifications area—

which users have viewed your profile. By the same token, other users will be notified when you view theirs.

CONNECTING ON LINKEDIN

When getting started on LinkedIn, you will have the option of finding and adding connections in a number of ways—through your email contact list, via others at your workplace or alma mater, or via other social media platforms. You can click the *My Network* button at the top of the page to view your connections.

Each time you do this, LinkedIn will suggest "people you may know" through mutual contacts of current connections, leaders in your industry, or a variety of other factors. To connect with anyone on that list, or anyone you might simply search for, just click the *Connect* button. That will send a notification to the person that you'd like to connect. If they accept, you're connected!

You will see posts shared by your connections, stories they might have Liked, and generally any news that happens to those in your network. For example, job changes, work anniversaries, and even birthdays.

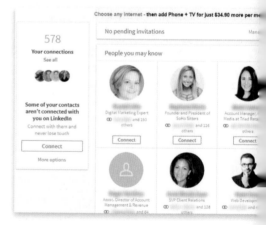

Under the *My Network* button you will find professional connections you may know from your employment or education history, social media, or email.

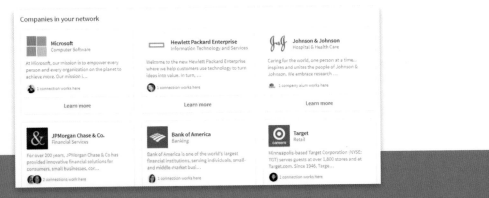

SEARCHING FOR JOBS

While LinkedIn is a terrific networking tool for working people in all lines of business, it is also a great place to start looking for a new job. If you click the *Jobs* button at the top of the page, you will see a number of options when it comes to searching for that next gig.

You can browse through openings at companies in your network. You can click a button that allows recruiters to see your profile and areas of expertise. You can also simply search for jobs based on any number of criteria such as title, location, and seniority level.

If finding a new job is at the top of your to-do list, it might be a smart idea to consider paying for LinkedIn Premium. For a monthly fee, it gives you several job-hunting advantages like rating where your profile falls among candidates for a role and the ability to contact job posters directly through a feature called InMail.

WHAT IS PINTEREST?

Within just a year of its launch in 2010, Pinterest had become one of the 10 largest social media sites on the web and was listed among the best sites on the internet by *Time* magazine. It was described by CEO Ben Silbermann as an inspiring "catalog of ideas" rather than a sharing network based on text or images. The idea was for people to share ideas and inspiration that would spark others to go out and join in the fun.

GETTING STARTED ON PINTEREST

As with most social media platforms, getting signed up is easy. You can use your Facebook or Google

logins if using a Chrome browser, or you can simply give your email address and choose a password. You'll be signed up in no time.

Pinterest will then ask you to identify some of your interests. You will notice that it touts the "discovering of new ideas." That's what Pinterest is all about. The more interests you identify, the broader the range of ideas you will see on each visit to the site.

PIN IT = SAVE

In 2016, Pinterest renamed the *Pin It* button *Save*. The purpose remains the same, however, and is core to the use of the site. You can add this functionality to your web browser, which makes it easy to Save, or Pin, and share images or ideas with other Pinterest users who share your passions.

PINTEREST FEATURES

Many of Pinterest's features resemble those of other social media platforms. Commenting and liking, for instance. You can add your kudos and "two cents" to the pins of others and join in the conversation.

However, Pinterest offers other functions that are unique to its platform. Some of those features are outlined here.

Boards: Boards are collections of Pins around a certain topic. Users can create and share any number of Boards made up of Pins they have collected.